Also by Jaroslaw Jankowski

Why Are We So Different?
Your Guide to the 16 Personality Types

Why are we so very different from one another? Why do we organise our lives in such disparate ways? Why are our modes of assimilating information so varied? Why are our approaches to decision-making so diverse? Why are our forms of relaxing and 'recharging our batteries' so dissimilar?

Your Guide to the 16 Personality Types will help you to understand both yourselves and other people better. It will aid you not only in avoiding any number of traps, but also in making the most of your personal potential, as well as in taking the right decisions about your education and career and in building healthy relationships with others.

The book contains the ID16™© Personality Test, which will enable you to determine your own personality type. It also offers a comprehensive description of each of the sixteen types.

The Innovator

**Your Guide
to the ENTP Personality Type**

The ID16™© Personality Types series

JAROSLAW JANKOWSKI
M.Ed., EMBA

This is a book which can help you exploit your potential more fully, build healthy relationships with other people and make the right decisions about your education and career. However, it should not be considered to be a substitute for expert physiological or psychiatric consultation. Neither the author nor the publisher accept any responsibility whatsoever for any detrimental effects which may result from the inappropriate use of this book.

ID16™© is an independent typology developed by Polish educator and manager Jaroslaw Jankowski and grounded in Carl Gustav Jung's theory. It should not be confused with the personality typologies and tests proposed by other authors or offered by other institutions.

Original title: Twój typ osobowości: Innowator (ENTP)
Translated from the Polish by Caryl Swift
Proof reading: Lacrosse | experts in translation
Layout editing by Zbigniew Szalbot

Published by LOGOS MEDIA

© Jaroslaw Jankowski 2016-2023
All rights reserved

Paperback: ISBN 978-83-7981-072-7
EPUB: ISBN 978-83-7981-073-4
MOBI: ISBN 978-83-7981-074-1

Contents

Contents 5

Preface 7

ID16™© and Jungian Personality Typology 9

The Innovator (ENTP) 14

    The Personality in a Nutshell 14

    General character traits 16

    Socially 24

    Work and career paths 29

    Potential strengths and weaknesses 33

    Personal development 36

    Well-known figures 38

The ID16™© Personality Types in a Nutshell 41

- The Administrator (ESTJ) 41
- The Advocate (ESFJ) 43
- The Animator (ESTP) 44
- The Artist (ISFP) 45
- The Counsellor (ENFJ) 46
- The Director (ENTJ) 48
- The Enthusiast (ENFP) 49
- The Idealist (INFP) 50
- The Innovator (ENTP) 52
- The Inspector (ISTJ) 53
- The Logician (INTP) 54
- The Mentor (INFJ) 56
- The Practitioner (ISTP) 57
- The Presenter (ESFP) 58
- The Protector (ISFJ) 60
- The Strategist (INTJ) 61

Additional information 63

- The four natural inclinations 63
- The approximate percentage of each personality type in the world population 65
- The approximate percentage of women and men of each personality type in the world population 66

Bibliography 67

Preface

The work in your hands is a compendium of knowledge on the *innovator*. It forms part of the *ID16™© Personality Types* series, which consists of sixteen books on the individual personality types and *Who Are You? The ID16™© Personality Test*, an introduction to the ID16™© independent personality typology, which is based on the theory developed by Carl Gustav Jung.

As you explore this book on the *innovator*, you will find the answer to a number of crucial questions:
- How do *innovators* think and what do they feel? How do they make decisions? How do they solve problems? What makes them anxious? What do they fear? What irritates them?
- Which personality types are they happy to encounter on their road through life and which ones do they avoid? What kind of

friends, life partners and parents do they make? How do others perceive them?
- What are their vocational predispositions? What sort of work environment allows them to function most effectively? Which careers best suit their personality type?
- What are their strengths and what do they need to work on? How can they make the most of their potential and avoid pitfalls?
- Which famous people correspond to the *innovator*'s profile?

The book also contains the most essential information about the ID16™© typology.

We sincerely hope that it will help you in coming to know yourself and others better.

ID16™© and Jungian Personality Typology

ID16™© numbers among what are referred to as Jungian personality typologies, which draw on the theories developed by Carl Gustav Jung (1875-19161), a Swiss psychiatrist and psychologist and a pioneer of the 'depth psychology' approach.

On the basis of many years of research and observation, Jung came to the conclusion that the differences in people's attitudes and preferences are far from random. He developed a concept which is highly familiar to us today: the division of people into extroverts and introverts. In addition, he distinguished four personality functions, which form two opposing pairs: sensing-intuition and thinking-feeling. He also established that one function is dominant in each pair. He became convinced that each and every person's dominant functions are fixed and independent of external conditions and that, together, what they form is a personality type.

In 1938, two American psychiatrists, Horace Gray and Joseph Wheelwright, created the first personality test based on Jung's theories. It was designed to make it possible to determine the dominant functions within the three dimensions described by Jung, namely, **extraversion-introversion**, **sensing-intuition** and **thinking-feeling**. That first test became the inspiration for other researchers. In 1942, again in America, Isabel Briggs Myers and Katherine Briggs began using their own personality test, broadening Gray's and Wheelwright's classic, three-dimensional model to include a fourth: **judging-perceiving**. The majority of subsequent personality typologies and tests drawing on Jung's theories also take that fourth dimension into account. They include the American typology published by David W. Keirsey in 1978 and the personality test developed in the nineteen seventies by Aušra Augustinavičiūtė, a Lithuanian psychologist. Over the following decades, other European researchers followed in their footsteps, creating more four-dimensional personality typologies and tests for use in personal coaching and career counselling.

ID16™© figures among that group. An independent typology developed by Polish educator and manager Jaroslaw Jankowski, it was published in the first decade of the twenty-first century. ID16™© is based on Carl Jung's classic theory and, like other contemporary Jungian typologies, it follows a four-dimensional path, terming those dimensions the **four natural inclinations**. These inclinations are dichotomous in nature and the picture they provide gives us information regarding a person's personality type. Analysis of the first inclination is intended to determine the dominant **source of life energy**, this being either the exterior or the interior world. Analysis of the second inclination defines the dominant **mode of assimilating information**, which occurs via the senses or via intuition. Analysis of the third inclination supplies a description of the **decision-making mode**, where either mind or heart is dominant, while analysis of the fourth inclination produces a definition of the dominant **lifestyle** as either organised or spontaneous. The combination of all these natural inclinations results in **sixteen possible personality types**.

One remarkable feature of the ID16™© typology is its practical dimension. It describes the individual personality types in action – at work, in daily life and in interpersonal relations. It neither concentrates on the internal dynamics of personality nor does it undertake any theoretical attempts at explaining or commenting on invisible, interior processes. The focus is turned more toward the ways in which a given personality type manifests itself externally and how it affects the surrounding world. This emphasis on the social aspect of personality places ID16™© somewhat closer to the previously mentioned typology developed by Aušra Augustinavičiūtė.

Each of the ID16™© personality types is the result of a given person's natural inclinations. There is nothing evaluative or judgemental about ascribing a person to a given type, though. No particular personality type is 'better' or 'worse' than any other. Each type is quite simply different and each has its own potential strengths and weaknesses. ID16™© makes it possible to identify and describe those differences. It helps us to understand ourselves and discover our place in the world.

Familiarity with our personality profile enables us to make full use of our potential and work on the areas which might cause us trouble. It is an invaluable aid in everyday life, in solving problems, in building healthy relationships with other people and in making decisions relating to our education and careers.

Determining personality is a process which is neither arbitrary nor mechanical in nature. As the 'owner and user' of our personality, each and every one of us is fully capable of defining which type we belong to. The individual's role is thus pivotal. This self-identification can be achieved either by analysing the descriptions of the ID16™© personality types and steadily narrowing down the fields of choice or by taking the short cut provided by the ID16™© Personality Test.[1] The role played by each 'personality user' is equally crucial when it comes to the test, given that the outcome depends entirely on the answers they provide.

Identifying personality types helps us to know both ourselves and others. Nonetheless, it should not be treated as some kind of future-determining oracle. No personality type can ever justify our weaknesses or poor interpersonal relationships. It might, however, help us to understand their causes!

ID16™© treats personality type not as a static, genetic, pre-determined condition, but as a product

---

[1] The test can be found in *Why Are We So Different? Your Guide to the 16 Personality Types* by Jaroslaw Jankowski.

of innate and acquired characteristics. As such, it is a concept which neither diminishes free will nor engages in pigeonholing people. What it does is open up new perspectives for us, encouraging us to work on ourselves and indicating the areas where that work is most needed.

The Innovator (ENTP)

THE ID16™© PERSONALITY TYPOLOGY

The Personality in a Nutshell

Life motto: How about trying a different approach…?

In brief, *innovators* …

are inventive, original and independent. Optimistic, energetic and enterprising, they are people of action who love being at the centre of events and solving 'insoluble' problems. Their thoughts are turned to the future and they are curious about the world and visionary by nature. Open to new concepts and ideas, they enjoy new experiences and experiments and have the ability to identify the connections between separate events.

Innovators are spontaneous, communicative and self-assured. However, they tend to overestimate their own possibilities and have problems with seeing things through to the end. They are also inclined to be impatient and to take risks.

The *innovator's* four natural inclinations:

- source of life energy: the exterior world
- mode of assimilating information: intuition
- decision-making mode: the mind
- lifestyle: spontaneous

Similar personality types:

- the Director
- the Logician
- the Strategist

Statistical data:

- *innovators* constitute between three and five per cent of the global community
- men predominate among *innovators* (70 per cent)
- Israel is an example of a nation corresponding to the *innovator's* profile[2]

The Four-Letter Code

In terms of Jungian personality typology, the universal four-letter code for the *innovator* is ENTP.

---

[2] What this means is not that all the residents of Israel fall within this personality type, but that Israeli society as a whole possesses a great many of the character traits typical of the *innovator*.

General character traits

Perceptive and resourceful, with coruscating minds, *innovators* feel completely at home in a world of complicated systems and complex theories. A creative approach to problems and the ability to multitask are an inherent part of their nature. Curious about the world and the phenomena which occur in it, every kind of mystery intrigues them. They value concepts and theories which can be translated into practical action, for instance in helping to solve specific problems, simplify life or make it possible to increase the effectiveness of their own or other people's work. By the same token, they have difficulty in understanding those who delight in purely theoretical solutions.

Problem solving

When *innovators* analyse a problem, they study the bigger picture, looking at the issue from various angles. Given their multiplanar analysis, they often perceive more than others and their deliberations and ideas will normally take on the form of cohesive systems. During a crisis, while other people can see nothing but the negative aspects of the situation, *innovators* are capable of spotting the possibilities and opportunities. On the other hand, when the majority are swept up in general euphoria and delight, it will be the *innovators* who display the ability to foresee potential dangers and future problems – and their assessments of the situation in question will usually be spot on.

They identify the essence of problems more clearly than others and derive enormous satisfaction from solving them. Their approach to tasks is innovative and unconventional, while their nature is to strive for thoroughgoing, systemic and far-reaching solutions which get to the crux of the matter. They tend to implement provisional solutions that either camouflage an issue or eliminate it for a while, but fail to address and remove the cause. In general, they are demanding of themselves and of others and will throw themselves wholeheartedly into accomplishing tasks they believe in, without thought of the time they devote to that end.

When they come up against a problem, *innovators* are quick to get to the heart of the issue and take whatever action is necessary. At the same time, they are guided by logical and objective reasoning and are not taken in by appearances. In changing conditions and circumstances, they are equally fast in reacting to a new situation and revising their previous decisions accordingly. When they launch into action, they will sometimes neglect the 'human element' and, while they will give consideration to whether or not they have the right to proceed in a certain way and will also ask themselves if the decision to do so is a rational one, they are less often interested in how their behaviour will be received by other people. This attitude means that, at times, what they do can be perceived as lacking in humanity or unethical. On the other hand, it would be difficult to accuse them of acting irrationally or unlawfully.

View of the world

Innovators are capable of identifying the principles governing the world and the connections linking apparently disparate phenomena. In combining separate elements, they create cohesive systems.

They also take note of repetitive patterns of human behaviour and are able to formulate theories explaining those patterns. Viewing life as a jigsaw, they constantly seek the missing parts and are delighted when the separate pieces start coming together to form a whole. By the same token, discovering the hitherto unknown gives them greater satisfaction than the knowledge and experience they already possess. They have the ability to make use both of other people's experience and of whatever means and tools are available to them; however, they will often do so in an innovative and unconventional way. By nature, they are superb strategists and planners.

Thinking

Innovators strive for perfection. With their thoughts fixed firmly on the future, they reflect on existing needs, unsolved problems and potential opportunities. Their minds are always intensively busy, even when they themselves are not, and they are constantly gripped not only by creative tension, but also by a highly particular sense of restlessness – after all, they do have a consuming desire to improve and rationalise existing solutions. New challenges give them added energy and new ideas, and theories which make it possible to take a fresh look at existing problems fill them with excitement. They will always spot potential and opportunity, no matter where or when.

Tasks

As a rule, *innovators* are characterised by their creativity and inventive approach to their tasks, whatever their job may be. New discoveries and pioneering technological solutions fascinate them and they are often bold innovators themselves ... hence the name for this personality type. Quick to warm to new ideas, they have the ability to fire others with their enthusiasm and, as a result, have no difficulty in finding colleagues to support them in bringing venturesome visions and projects to life. At times, though, they tend to overestimate what they can manage to achieve. In general, the newest challenges will exert the strongest tug on their attention, abating their enthusiasm for previous tasks.

A widespread problem amongst *innovators* is the fact that they are easily distracted; their fascination with a whole host of things and their burning desire to bring a mass of ideas to fruition mean that they are sometimes incapable of seeing anything at all through to the end, a situation which often drives them into a state of furious frustration. They are also irritated by everyday routine activities which, in their view, limit them and rob them of valuable time.

Enthusiasms

Innovators are frequently interested in technological novelties. When new devices which have yet to be universally adopted hit the market, *innovators* will reach for them earlier and more readily than others. Among their friends and acquaintances, they are regarded as experts, since, by the time the majority of people have concluded that a new piece of equipment or device is worthy of interest, *innovators* will often already have extensive experience in using it. Moreover, it is rare indeed for them to stick to availing themselves solely of its main functions; they are usually most likely to explore the more advanced options and even experiment in order to try and employ it in ways which are not only unconventional, but may well not have been foreseen by the manufacturer.

This can, of course, lead to their damaging the device, particularly when they are young; though, on the other hand, they often improve on it, introducing valuable innovations or adding new functions. With time, many *innovators* become not only rationalists, but also the creators of projects, as well as designers and inventors. Their innovativeness also makes itself manifest in creating new work organisation systems, new business concepts and new concepts for explaining the phenomena occurring in the world.

In general, *innovators* love travelling and exploring new places, different cultures and diverse ways of looking at the world. They are open to atypical, out-of-the-ordinary and unconventional solutions and adapt with ease to changing circumstances and conditions. New experiences inspire them and spur them to act. They are not afraid to experiment and their approach to tasks is often absolutely new and fresh. By the same token, people who believe that the best way to solve problems is by clinging to orthodox, tried and tested methods are a source of puzzlement to them.

In the face of change

Innovators are drawn to change. The vision and possibility of beginning life afresh, making the most of new chances and grasping new opportunities is something that inspires them. They are more likely than most to carry out a searching revision of their existing system of values, give themselves over to a new concept or switch their lives onto a wholly new course. With no fear of the new and unknown, the fact that no one has ever done what they are doing or that very few share their views is no obstacle to them.

They enjoy being 'the first' and feel completely at home in the role of groundbreaker and guide, blazing the trail, pointing the way and leading others towards new horizons. *Innovators* are simply not numbered among those who are quick to give up without really trying; instead, they see obstacles and limitations as a challenge and an inspiration to take action. Always happy to breathe life into new projects and pioneering solutions, they will pass the baton of post-implementation care on to others, while they themselves turn their focus to the next problem. As a rule, it is the initial, conceptual phase and launching of a project that interest them, and they cope badly with routine work involving repetitive activities.

Attitude to others

Innovators respect others, particularly those who are capable of taking up challenges, wrestling with adversities, confronting difficulties head on, fighting in a just cause and consciously exposing themselves to the criticism, resistance and incomprehension of those around them as a result. They value people who have the courage to introduce unpopular, though essential, changes, shake the existing order and question the *status quo*. However, they have trouble tolerating errors and negligence on the part of others and are impatient with those who have less knowledge and experience than they do and who fail to keep pace with them.

Accepting that other people cannot see what they themselves deem patently obvious is also problematic for them, as is understanding those who are passive and display no initiative. They tend to perceive a lack of enthusiasm as a manifestation of passivity or laziness, a view which is often both erroneous and unjust. Incapable, on the whole, of keeping their calm when they see a job done badly, they will normally call attention to the issue at once, pointing out the mistakes to those responsible and endeavouring to correct their behaviour. Other people's injudicious and illogical decisions are another source of irritation to them.

As others see them

Innovators are perceived as decisive, powerful and sure that they are right. In general, they also have a reputation for being creative, rational and competent. Others know that, in the face of serious problems, they can be counted on to provide help and advice. However, their self-assurance is often taken as arrogance and self-aggrandisement.

A great many people are irritated not only by the fact that *innovators* like to be the centre of attention and have things their own way, but also by their belief that they are always in the right. There are also those who criticise them for their want of empathy, unreasonable demands and insensitivity to the needs of others. Their love of change and unceasing pursuit of the new can sometimes mean that they are seen as inconsistent, chaotic and lacking in perseverance.

Communication

Innovators possess excellent oral communication skills, being able to describe complex problems and theories in a simple, comprehensible fashion. They express themselves extremely precisely, making conscious use of carefully selected words. Generally self-assured, they unhesitatingly voice their convictions in public, even when they are in the minority. They make for difficult partners in polemics, since they are capable of presenting their arguments in a way which is both dazzling and persuasive, and of giving convincing proof of the rightness of their views.

A love of contradicting and polemicising, even for the sheer pleasure of it, is second nature to them. Capable of providing snap answers to questions and refuting arguments, they have no fear of criticism, conflict or unfavourable reactions from others. They are also hard to hurt and, in general, are unaware of the fact that not everyone has the same high threshold of tolerance for critical commentary as they do. As a result, they will often wound people with their bluntly expressed remarks and may well interrupt them in the middle of a sentence. Behaviour of this kind on the part of *innovators* tends to fluster and dishearten those who are less self-assured and engenders a reluctance to enter into conversation with them.

In the face of stress

On the whole, *innovators* derive pleasure from their work. However, the enthusiasm with which they launch themselves into accomplishing a task will frequently disrupt the balance between 'work, rest and play'. Overwork and long-term stress can lead them to become stubborn and unbending and they may well begin to walk all over everyone in their efforts to accomplish what they have planned. They can also react to stress with an exaggerated fear of illness and suffering or with a sense of being isolated, alienated, cast aside and forgotten.

Socially

Open to the world and other people, *innovators* are approachable and easy to get to know. Drawn to wherever the action is, they find being isolated and alone for any length of time hard to bear. They relate to others with ease, spontaneity and flexibility, enjoy getting to know new people and striking up acquaintanceships, and make excellent hosts at get-togethers and gatherings.

Innovators adore surprises and spontaneous fun, adapting to whatever the situation may be with no trouble at all. On the other hand, they are lost in the world of human emotions and feelings and those of a more emotional and affective nature might take them to be cold and insensitive or even accuse them of treating people instrumentally by seeing them as sources of information or problem-solving tools, for instance.

Delighting in disputes and debates, *innovators* handle confrontation well and appreciate those who are capable of fighting in defence of their own views, an attitude which often scares away people who have no driving need of that kind. Seen from the other side of the coin, their unwillingness to engage in confrontation might well be read by *innovators* as a sign of weakness or a lack of conviction in the opinions they profess.

Amongst friends

Good and friendly relations with people are important to *innovators*. What lies at the heart of their bonds of friendship is exchanging information, sharing concepts and ideas and working together to solve problems. Meeting up with other people gives them energy, helps them to develop and acts as a positive spur.

Innovators love inspiring conversations with people who matter to them and are capable of discussing anything and everything; as a rule, they acknowledge no topic as taboo and have no fear that a discussion might take a dangerous turn, such as impelling them to verify their previous convictions, for example. They enjoy spending time with people who have a wide range of interests, help them to look at problems from another angle and, like them, welcome new ideas and challenges. They themselves are equally as happy to share their reflections and knowledge. Their openness, flexibility and spontaneity make them sought-after conversationalists and company.

Their friendships are most often formed with people who are similar to themselves, distinctive for their intelligence, inventiveness and sparkling minds; they thus tend only to turn their attention to others when they show an interest in their ideas and reflections. Many an *innovator* feels that friendships should enrich people and help them to develop, but that, if they exhaust their potential, they can be brought to a close. *Directors*, *logicians*, *animators* and other *innovators* are most frequently encountered amongst their friends, with *protectors*, *advocates* and *artists* appearing most rarely.

As life partners

As life partners, *innovators* take their obligations very seriously. They bring optimism, enthusiasm and spontaneity to their relationships and, given their love of new experiences and experiments, boredom is unlikely to threaten their partners. Being people of action, they show their devotion not so much by way of tender gestures and warm words as through doing something concrete. Their nature renders them rather insensitive to their partner's feelings and they can often be unaware of their emotional needs; they may love them dearly and yet, at one and the same time, have absolutely no grasp whatsoever of what they are experiencing and feeling, or of their emotional state. However, with a little effort, they can change this and, if they are in a relationship with a person of a romantic disposition, making that effort is an absolute must!

Innovators themselves have few emotional needs. They like to know that they are important to, and loved by, their life partner, but they do not, as a rule, expect endearing words, compliments and frequent assurances of their love and affection. Their positive attitude to confrontations and disputes can be a serious problem for romantically inclined and sensitive partners and it may often be the case that they will hurt those closest to them with their remarks or critical comments, yet have not the slightest idea that they have caused them pain. On the whole, they like to be right and frequently have a problem with admitting to their mistakes or weaknesses. Expressing their own feelings and emotions is also hard for them.

During periods of intensive work or particular stress, they can make difficult partners, as they become stubborn and may fail to take the needs of others into consideration or might even start exerting pressure on them. *Innovators* warm to new ideas rapidly and, once a task has fired their enthusiasm, they will roll up their sleeves and get working on it without further ado. Being capable of devoting all their energy and time to that, what may then ensue are problems in their relationships, particularly when their partner neither shares their enthusiasm nor understands their engrossment. This burning engagement is something they might well carry over into matters of family life; indeed, they have a tendency to treat problems and tasks in that respect as projects which need to be accomplished. What can happen, though, is that their enthusiasm dies down when new tasks and more exciting challenges appear on the horizon. Although sincere in their resolve, they have a struggle in keeping promises they have made and, after ideas have initially fired them up, they find it tough to see them through to the end. At the same time, their characteristic thirst for new impressions and their love of adventure and experiment pose a potential threat to the stability of their relationships. *Innovators* long for good relationships and, as a rule, they will not seek a way out of them. However, they are capable of putting an end to them if, in their opinion, they have become damaging and destructive.

The natural candidates for an *innovator's* life partner are people of a personality type akin to their own: *directors*, *logicians* or *strategists*. Building mutual understanding and harmonious relations will be easier in a union of that kind. Nonetheless, experience has taught us that people are also capable of creating happy and successful relationships despite what would seem to be an evident typological incompatibility. Moreover, the differences between two partners can lend added dynamics to a relationship and engender personal development. Indeed, for many people, this is a prospect that appears more attractive than the vision of a harmonious relationship wherein concord and full, mutual understanding hold sway.

As parents

As parents, *innovators* have a superb understanding of children's curiosity about the world. In a sense, they themselves always have something of the child in them, and they never lose that curiosity and love of experimentation, adventure and fun. They endeavour to provide their offspring with as many experiences and stimuli as they possibly can, happily organising expeditions and carefree fun with them and deriving just as much joy from the activities as the children do. They will generally instil the ability to think critically in them and will strive to bring them up to become independent, self-sufficient people capable of objectively evaluating facts and making rational and logical decisions.

Their unpredictability can be a problem; they will sometimes make their children a promise or set something up with them, only to face difficulty in following through on it later. They are also easily distracted. When a new vision sweeps them up and they commit themselves wholly to bringing it to fruition, they may well forget their offspring's needs or arrangements they have previously made. Their adult children appreciate the way their *innovator* parent respected their independence, supported them in developing their enthusiasms and taught them to be self-sufficient. They will also have fond memories of family outings and experiments, along with every precious moment spent having fun together.

Work and career paths

Innovators like work which creates an opportunity for experimentation. They excel at pioneering tasks and will often employ methods which others have not dared to try, reaching for new solutions or applying those which already exist in an innovative way and creating an entirely fresh quality as a result. They enjoy 'unconventional' tasks and will readily work in the 'line of fire'.

Skills and stumbling blocks

Motivated by their awareness that unsolved problems and untapped potential opportunities exist, *innovators* face their greatest problem when confronted by work demanding that they perform routine, repetitive and schematic activities. In general, they also have no fondness for tasks which demand a great deal of preparation. On the other hand, they possess excellent improvisational skills and are quick to adapt to new situations. They are capable of multitasking and reconciling various responsibilities. However, with their love of experiment and change, they will often forget about previous arrangements and duties in the face of new and exciting tasks and they also have trouble with working systematically and seeing things through to the end.

As part of a team

Innovators enjoy working in a group. They normally establish good relationships with people and are well liked. However, their preference is for tasks demanding a creative approach and problem-solving skills rather than empathy and the ability to discern human emotions, feelings and needs. They are happiest working with people who are experts in their field and are open both to experiments and to innovative and risky solutions. The reverse side of the coin is the sheer suffering they endure when they have to work with those for whom 'the old ways are the best' and who favour 'tried and trusted' methods and cling tightly to instructions, guidelines and rules.

Tasks

In general, *innovators* find conventional thinking and rigid, fossilised, bureaucratic structures hard to bear. Arguments grounded in tradition carry no weight with them and, if they view a solution as inadequate and insufficiently effective, they are liable to discard it, regardless of who introduced it and how long it has been in place, an approach which sometimes earns them a reputation as dangerous revolutionaries and subversives.

They are usually unwilling to acquiesce to any kind of regulations or instructions and often treat restrictions, be they institutional or legal, as obstacles on the road to achieving their aims; indeed, if they consider a regulation to be unreasonable, pointless or absurd, they are quite capable of consciously ignoring it. They will sometimes mete out the same treatment to people who hamper them in bringing their ideas to life. In fact, when they are firmly convinced that something is essential, they are capable of putting pressure on those who stand in their way. However, despite having a destructive impact on others, their pertinacity frequently determines their success.

Innovators fit in best in companies which give their employees freedom in carrying out their tasks, allow them to experiment, encourage them to seek new solutions, and support creativity and innovativeness. They enjoy environments where discussion on any and every topic is permitted and everyone is free to air their own convictions.

Views on workplace hierarchy

Innovators like and value superiors who provide their staff with freedom of action and single out knowledge, experience, competence and professionalism. Their respect is for people who are true experts in their field and have no fear of experimenting – for instance, by giving up the methods applied thus far in favour of new and more innovative solutions. Their ideal bosses will evaluate employees with due consideration for their creativity, ideas and the tasks they perform, rather than giving weight to the amount of paperwork they get through and their scrupulous adherence to procedures.

In positions of authority themselves, they will apply this method of assessing those under them and will most readily select colleagues who are capable of making independent decisions, know what needs to be done in a given situation and require neither constant instructions and pointers nor close supervision. They find subordinates who constantly need their hands held intensely irritating. *Innovators* are not the kind of people who shower their employees with compliments in order to enhance their sense of well-being and make work a happy place. Nonetheless, they do value their achievements and reward measurable success.

Natural leaders and visionaries, *innovators* are able to point the way, make others aware of existing possibilities, inspire them, give them added courage and infect them with enthusiasm and faith that their undertakings will succeed. However, when they hold supervisory or managerial positions, they need the strong support of assistants or secretaries to whom they can assign all their practical, routine duties.

Professions

Knowledge of our own personality profile and natural preferences provides us with invaluable help in choosing the optimal path in our professional careers. Experience has shown that, while *innovators* are perfectly able to work and find fulfilment in a range of fields, their personality type naturally predisposes them to the following fields and professions:

- acting
- artistic director
- computer programmer
- computer systems analyst
- credit analyst
- engineer
- entrepreneur
- estate agent
- events organiser
- financial advisor
- infrastructure / property developer
- investment and stockbroking
- journalist

- lawyer
- logistics
- marketing
- musician
- photographer
- politician
- press spokesperson
- project coordinator
- psychiatrist
- psychologist
- public relations
- reporter
- sales representative
- scientist
- urban and rural planning
- visual artist
- writer

Potential strengths and weaknesses

Like any other personality type, *innovators* have their potential strengths and weaknesses, and this potential can be cultivated in a variety of ways. *Innovators'* personal happiness and professional fulfilment depend on whether they make the most of the 'pluses' offered by their personality type and face up to its inherent dangers. Here, then, is a SUMMARY of those 'pluses' and dangers:

Potential strengths

Innovators are creative, optimistic and energetic, with the ability both to fire others with enthusiasm and faith in their success and to stir them into action.

Nimble-minded, they are logical, rational and insusceptible to manipulation by others. Assimilating complex concepts and theories presents them with no problems. They have a natural curiosity about the world and are able to understand the phenomena which occur in it and the mechanisms driving people's behaviour, to identify the connections and relationships between different events and to look at problems from various angles. When opportunities and possibilities emerge, *innovators* are quicker than most to spot them, just as they are to foresee potential, future dangers.

Enterprising by nature, they like new concepts and pioneering ideas and will readily reach for innovative solutions and methods. Being exceptionally creative and bold, they are able to solve problems in unconventional, original ways and they have no fear of experimenting. They are always happy to learn something new and undertake fresh challenges, enjoy solving complex problems and are not afraid to take risks. Extremely flexible and capable of adapting to new circumstances, they enjoy both the company of others and working in a group. In general, they possess outstanding communication skills, being capable of expressing their thoughts and voicing their opinions clearly and comprehensibly. Neither criticism nor confrontation frightens them and they cope well in difficult, conflict situations. They strive for self-improvement and are always willing to help others to develop.

Potential weaknesses

With their love of change and experiment, pursuit of the new and focus on the latest and most powerful stimuli, *innovators* have far less difficulty in beginning something than they do in seeing it through to the end. They are also easily distracted and their enthusiasm for the tasks they have started vanishes when new problems and challenges appear on the horizon. This means that they drop numerous fascinating ideas at the conceptual stage without even trying to implement them in reality. They also struggle with organising their time, applying self-discipline, making decisions, keeping promises and sticking to deadlines. Defining priorities and then bringing their activities in line with them is also problematic for them. They cope badly with tasks which require them to adhere to strict procedures and follow instructions to the letter.

Another problem which frequently crops up among *innovators* is their impatience with less experienced people who need guidelines, prompting and pointers. Their boldness and unwavering faith that they will succeed may well lead to their making overly risky moves and employing excessively radical solutions. They are liable to overestimate their own possibilities and disregard their limitations. Both their inability to perceive the emotions and feelings of others and the difficulty they have in expressing their own can give rise to problems in their relationships with those closest to them. At the same time, with their confrontational approach, critical comments, general determination to have things their own way and love of dispute and polemic, they are likely to hurt and discourage more sensitive people and may even frighten them away.

Personal development

Innovators' personal development depends on the extent to which they make use of their natural potential and surmount the dangers inherent in their personality type. What follows are some practical indicators which, together, form a specific guide that we might call *The Innovator's Ten Commandments*.

Learn to manage your time and set priorities

Enthusiasm is your main driving force. Nonetheless, listing priorities, establishing time frames and planning out a job are not in the least the same thing as forging chains to shackle your creativity, fetter your activities and encumber you as you carry out the task. Perish the thought! They are tools and when you use them properly, they will help you achieve your sought-after goals.

Be more practical

Give some thought to the practical aspects of your theories and ideas. To make the very most of their potential, try persuading other people to come round to them and considering ways of turning them into reality. Why leave the fruits of your work to languish, neglected and unaccomplished to the full?

When you start something, see it through to the end

You launch into new things enthusiastically, but have problems with finishing what you have already started. Try sorting out what is most important to you and deciding how you want to accomplish it.

Then knuckle down and turn your back firmly on all those tempting distractions! Keep your eyes fixed on your priorities and stop letting yourself be distracted by less important matters.

Admit that you can make mistakes

Things may be more complex than they seem to you. You might not always be in the right. Bring that thought to the forefront of your mind before you start accusing others or pointing out their mistakes and reproaching them.

Criticise less

Not everyone has your ability to handle constructive criticism. In many cases, dispensing it frankly can have a destructive effect. Studies have shown that praising positive behaviour, albeit limited, motivates people more than criticising negative conduct.

Stop discarding other people's ideas and opinions

Just because other people's ideas and opinions conflict with your own, this does not automatically mean that they are wrong. Before you judge them as valueless, give them some serious consideration and try to understand them.

Focus on the positive

Instead of concentrating on what is missing, on mistakes, on logical contradictions and on questioning other people's good intentions, learn to identify the positive and turn your gaze to the bright side of life.

Be more understanding

Show others more warmth. Remember that not everyone should be assigned the same tasks, because not everyone is skilled in the same fields. If others are unable to cope with a task, this is not always a sign of their ill will or laziness.

Remember important dates and anniversaries

Arrangements to meet people, the birthdays of those closest to you and family anniversaries may seem like rather trivial matters to you in comparison to whatever it is you are involved in. They matter a great deal to other people, though. So if you are incapable of remembering them, jot them down somewhere handy – and then remember to check those notes!

Praise others

Make the most of every occasion to appreciate other people, say something nice to them and praise them for something they have done. At work, value people not only for the job they do, but also for who they are. Then wait and see. The difference will come as a pleasant surprise!

Well-known figures

Below is a list of some well-known people who match the *innovator's* profile:

- **Lewis Carroll** (Charles Lutwidge Dodgson; 1832-1898); an English writer whose works include *Alice's Adventures in Wonderland*, he was also a mathematician and the author of around two hundred and fifty scholarly

works in the fields of mathematics, logic and cryptography.
- **Thomas Edison** (1847-1931); one of the world's best-known and most creative inventors, with more than a thousand patents to his name, including the light bulb and the phonograph, he was also an entrepreneur and the founder of a periodical entitled *Science*.
- **Nikola Tesla** (1856-1943); a Croatian inventor with one hundred and twelve patents to his name, he was also a poet and painter.
- **Theodore Roosevelt** (1858-1919); the 26th president of the United States, he received the Nobel Peace Prize.
- **Buckminster Fuller** (1895-1983); an American designer and architect, he was one of the pioneers of high-tech architecture and the man who developed and patented the geodesic dome.
- **Walt Disney** (Walter Elias Disney; 1901-1966); an American film producer, director, screenwriter, animator, entrepreneur and philanthropist, he founded the Walt Disney Company and Disneyland.
- **Richard Phillips Feynman** (1918-1988); an American theoretical physicist and one of the primary contributors to the development of quantum electrodynamics, he was awarded the Nobel Prize in Physics.
- **Jeremy Brett** (Peter Jeremy William Huggins; 1933-1995); an English stage and screen actor whose filmography includes the *Adventures of Sherlock Holmes* TV series.

THE INNOVATOR

- **John Marwood Cleese** (born in 1939); an English actor, comedian, writer and producer whose filmography includes *A Fish Called Wanda*, he was one of the co-founders of the Monty Python team.
- **Roberto Benigni** (born in 1952); an Italian stage and screen actor, comedian, screenwriter and director whose filmography includes *Life Is Beautiful*.
- **James Francis Cameron** (born in 1954); a Canadian film director and producer, screenwriter, editor, engineer, inventor, deep-sea explorer and philanthropist whose filmography includes *The Terminator* and *Titanic*.
- **Tom Hanks** (Thomas Jeffrey Hanks; born in 1956); an American screen actor, director and producer whose filmography includes *Philadelphia*, his extensive list of awards includes Oscars, Golden Globes and Emmys.
- **Jamie Lee Curtis** (born in 1958); an American screen actress whose filmography includes *A Fish Called Wanda*, she is also a children's author and involved in various philanthropic causes.
- **Salma Hayek-Jimenez** (born in 1966); a Mexican-American screen actress whose filmography includes *Desperado*.
- **Celine Dion** (born in 1968); a Canadian singer, songwriter and entrepreneur whose album sales make her one of the best-selling artists in the history of music.

The ID16™© Personality Types in a Nutshell

The Administrator (ESTJ)

Life motto: We'll get the job done!

Administrators are hard-working, responsible and extremely loyal. Energetic and decisive, they value order, stability, security and clear rules. They are matter-of-fact and businesslike, logical, rational and practical and possess the capability to assimilate large amounts of detailed information.

Superb organisers, they are intolerant of ineffectuality, wastefulness and slothfulness. True to their convictions and direct in their contact with others, they present their point of view decisively and openly express critical opinions, sometimes hurting other people as a result.

The *administrator*'s four natural inclinations:

- source of life energy: the exterior world
- mode of assimilating information: via the senses
- decision-making mode: the mind
- lifestyle: organised

Similar personality types:

- the Animator
- the Inspector
- the Practitioner

Statistical data:

- *administrators* constitute between ten and thirteen per cent of the global community
- men predominate among *administrators* (60 per cent)
- the United States is an example of a nation corresponding to the *administrator's* profile[3]

Find out more!

The Administrator. Your Guide to the ESTJ Personality Type by Jaroslaw Jankowski

---

[3] What this means is not that all the residents of the USA fall within this personality type, but that American society as a whole possesses a great many of the character traits typical of the *administrator*.

The Advocate (ESFJ)

Life motto: How can I help you?

Advocates are well-organised, energetic and enthusiastic. Practical, responsible and conscientious, they are sincere and exceptionally gregarious.

Advocates are perceptive of human feelings, emotions and needs. They value harmony and find criticism and conflict difficult to bear. With their sensitivity to any and every manifestation of injustice, prejudice or detriment to another, they are genuinely interested in other people's problems and take real delight in helping them and tending to their needs, while often neglecting their own. They have a tendency to do everything for others and can be vulnerable to manipulation.

The *advocate*'s four natural inclinations:

- source of life energy: the exterior world
- mode of assimilating information: via the senses
- decision-making mode: the heart
- lifestyle: organised

Similar personality types:

- the Presenter
- the Protector
- the Artist

Statistical data:

- *advocates* constitute between ten and thirteen per cent of the global community

- women predominate among *advocates* (70 per cent)
- Canada is an example of a nation corresponding to the *advocate's* profile

Find out more!

The Advocate. Your Guide to the ESFJ Personality Type by Jaroslaw Jankowski

The Animator (ESTP)

Life motto: Let's DO something!

Animators are energetic, active and enterprising. Fond of the company of others, they have the ability to enjoy the moment and are spontaneous, flexible and open to change.

Animators are inspirers and instigators, spurring others to act. Being logical, rational and pragmatic realists, they are wearied by abstract concepts and solutions for the future. Their focus is on solving concrete problems in the here and now. They have difficulties with organising and planning and can be impulsive, acting first and thinking later.

The *animator's* four natural inclinations:

- source of life energy: the exterior world
- mode of assimilating information: via the senses
- decision-making mode: the mind
- lifestyle: spontaneous

Similar personality types:
- the Administrator
- the Practitioner
- the Inspector

Statistical data:
- *animators* constitute between six and ten per cent of the global community
- men predominate among *animators* (60 per cent)
- Australia is an example of a nation corresponding to the *animator's* profile

Find out more!
The Animator. Your Guide to the ESTP Personality Type by Jaroslaw Jankowski

The Artist (ISFP)

Life motto: Let's create something!

Artists are sensitive, creative and original, with a sense of the aesthetic and natural artistic talents. Independent in character, they follow their own system of values and are optimistic in outlook, with a positive approach to life and an ability to enjoy the moment.

Helping others is a source of joy to them. They find abstract theories tedious and would rather create reality than talk about it, although starting on something new comes more easily to them than finishing what they have already started. They have difficulty in voicing their own desires and needs.

The *artist's* four natural inclinations:

- source of life energy: the interior world
- mode of assimilating information: via the senses
- decision-making mode: the heart
- lifestyle: spontaneous

Similar personality types:

- the Protector
- the Presenter
- the Advocate

Statistical data:

- *artists* constitute between six and nine per cent of the global community
- women predominate among *artists* (60 per cent)
- China is an example of a nation corresponding to the *artist's* profile

Find out more!

The Artist. Your Guide to the ISFP Personality Type by Jaroslaw Jankowski

The Counsellor (ENFJ)

Life motto: My friends are my world

Counsellors are optimistic, enthusiastic and quick-witted. Courteous and tactful, they have an extraordinary gift for empathy and find joy in acting for the good of others, with no thought of themselves. They have the ability to influence other people, inspiring them, eliciting their hidden potential and giving them faith in their own powers. Radiating warmth, they draw others to them and often help them in solving their personal problems.

Counsellors can be over-trusting and have a tendency to view the world through rose-tinted glasses. With their focus on other people, they often forget about their own needs.

The *counsellor's* four natural inclinations:

- source of life energy: the exterior world
- mode of assimilating information: intuition
- decision-making mode: the heart
- lifestyle: organised

Similar personality types:

- the Enthusiast
- the Mentor
- the Idealist

Statistical data:

- *counsellors* constitute between three and five per cent of the global community
- women predominate among *counsellors* (80 per cent)
- France is an example of a nation corresponding to the *counsellor's* profile

Find out more!

The Counsellor. Your Guide to the ENFJ Personality Type by Jaroslaw Jankowski

The Director (ENTJ)

Life motto: I'll tell you what you need to do.

Directors are independent, active and decisive. Rational, logical and creative, when they analyse problems they look at the wider picture and are able to foresee the future consequences of human activities. They are characterised by optimism and a healthy sense of their own worth and are capable of transforming theoretical concepts into concrete, practical plans of action.

Visionaries, mentors and organisers, *directors* possess natural leadership skills. Their powerful personalities and direct and critical style can often have an intimidating effect, causing them problems in their interpersonal relationships.

The *director's* four natural inclinations:

- source of life energy: the exterior world
- mode of assimilating information: intuition
- decision-making mode: the mind
- lifestyle: organised

Similar personality types:

- the Innovator
- the Strategist
- the Logician

Statistical data:

- *directors* constitute between two and five per cent of the global community
- men predominate among *directors* (70 per cent)

- Holland is an example of a nation corresponding to the *director's* profile

Find out more!
The Director. Your Guide to the ENTJ Personality Type by Jaroslaw Jankowski

The Enthusiast (ENFP)

Life motto: We'll manage!

Enthusiasts are energetic, enthusiastic and optimistic. Capable of enjoying life and looking ahead to the future, they are dynamic, quick-witted and creative. They have a liking for people in general, value honest and genuine relationships and are warm, sincere and emotional. Criticism is something they handle badly. With their gift for empathy and ability to perceive people's needs, feelings and motives, they both inspire others and infect them with their own enthusiasm.

They love to be at the centre of events and are flexible and capable of improvising. Their inclination leads towards idealistic notions. Being easily distracted, they have problems with seeing things through to the end.

The *enthusiast's* four natural inclinations:
- source of life energy: the exterior world
- mode of assimilating information: intuition
- decision-making mode: the heart
- lifestyle: spontaneous

Similar personality types:
- the Counsellor
- the Idealist
- the Mentor

Statistical data:
- *enthusiasts* constitute between five and eight per cent of the global community
- women predominate among *enthusiasts* (60 per cent)
- Italy is an example of a nation corresponding to the *enthusiast's* profile

Find out more!

The Enthusiast. Your Guide to the ENFP Personality Type by Jaroslaw Jankowski

The Idealist (INFP)

Life motto: We CAN live differently.

Idealists are sensitive, loyal, and creative. Living in accordance with the values they hold is of immense importance to them and they both manifest an interest in the reality of the spirit and delve deeply into the mysteries of life. Wrapped up in the world's problems and open to the needs of other people, they prize harmony and balance.

Idealists are romantic; not only are they able to show love, but they also need warmth and affection themselves. With their outstanding ability to read other people's feelings and emotions, they build healthy, profound and enduring relationships. They feel that they are on very shaky ground in situations of conflict and have no real resistance to stress and criticism.

The *idealist's* four natural inclinations:

- source of life energy: the interior world
- mode of assimilating information: intuition
- decision-making mode: the heart
- lifestyle: spontaneous

Similar personality types:

- the Mentor
- the Enthusiast
- the Counsellor

Statistical data:

- *idealists* constitute between one and four per cent of the global community
- women predominate among *idealists* (60 per cent)
- Thailand is an example of a nation corresponding to the *idealist's* profile

Find out more!

The Idealist. Your Guide to the INFP Personality Type by Jaroslaw Jankowski

The Innovator (ENTP)

Life motto: How about trying a different approach…?

Innovators are inventive, original and independent. Optimistic, energetic and enterprising, they are people of action who love being at the centre of events and solving 'insoluble' problems. Their thoughts are turned to the future and they are curious about the world and visionary by nature. Open to new concepts and ideas, they enjoy new experiences and experiments and have the ability to identify the connections between separate events.

Innovators are spontaneous, communicative and self-assured. However, they tend to overestimate their own possibilities and have problems with seeing things through to the end. They are also inclined to be impatient and to take risks.

The *innovator's* four natural inclinations:

- source of life energy: the exterior world
- mode of assimilating information: intuition
- decision-making mode: the mind
- lifestyle: spontaneous

Similar personality types:

- the Director
- the Logician
- the Strategist

Statistical data:

- *innovators* constitute between three and five per cent of the global community

- men predominate among *innovators* (70 per cent)
- Israel is an example of a nation corresponding to the *innovator's* profile

Find out more!

The Innovator. Your Guide to the ENTP Personality Type by Jaroslaw Jankowski

The Inspector (ISTJ)

Life motto: *Duty first.*

Inspectors are people who can always be counted on. Well-mannered, punctual, reliable, conscientious and responsible, when they give their word, they keep it. Being analytical, methodical, systematic and logical by nature, they tend be seen as serious, cold and reserved. They prize calm, stability and order, have no fondness for change and like clear principles and concrete rules.

Inspectors are hard-working, persevering and capable of seeing things through to the end. As perfectionists, they try to exercise control over everything within their sphere and are sparing in their praise. They also underrate the importance of other people's feelings and emotions.

The *inspector's* four natural inclinations:

- source of life energy: the interior world
- mode of assimilating information: via the senses

- decision-making mode: the mind
- lifestyle: organised

Similar personality types:
- the Practitioner
- the Administrator
- the Animator

Statistical data:
- *inspectors* constitute between six and ten per cent of the global community
- men predominate among *inspectors* (60 per cent)
- Switzerland is an example of a nation corresponding to the *inspector's* profile

Find out more!

The Inspector. Your Guide to the ISTJ Personality Type by Jaroslaw Jankowski

The Logician (INTP)

Life motto: Above all else, seek to discover the truths about the world.

Logicians are original, resourceful and creative. With a love for solving problems of a theoretical nature, they are analytical, quick-witted, enthusiastically disposed towards new concepts and have the ability to connect individual phenomena, educing general rules and theories from them. Logical, exact and inquiring, they are quick to spot incoherence and inconsistency.

Logicians are independent, sceptical of existing solutions and authorities, tolerant and open to new challenges. When immersed in thought, they will sometimes lose touch with the outside world.

The *logician's* four natural inclinations:

- source of life energy: the interior world
- mode of assimilating information: intuition
- decision-making mode: the mind
- lifestyle: spontaneous

Similar personality types:

- the Strategist
- the Innovator
- the Director

Statistical data:

- *logicians* constitute between two and three per cent of the global community;
- men predominate among *logicians* (80 per cent)
- India is an example of a nation corresponding to the *logician's* profile

Find out more!

The Logician. Your Guide to the INTP Personality Type by Jaroslaw Jankowski

The Mentor (INFJ)

Life motto: The world CAN be a better place!

Mentors are creative and sensitive. With their gaze fixed firmly on the future, they spot opportunities and potential imperceptible to others. Idealists and visionaries, they are geared towards helping people and are conscientious, responsible and, at one and the same time, courteous, caring and friendly. They strive to understand the mechanisms governing the world and view problems from a wide perspective.

Superb listeners and observers, *mentors* are characterised by their extraordinary empathy, intuition and trust of people and are capable of reading the feelings and emotions of others. They find criticism and conflict difficult to bear and can come across as enigmatic.

The *mentor's* four natural inclinations:

- source of life energy: the interior world
- mode of assimilating information: intuition
- decision-making mode: the heart
- lifestyle: organised

Similar personality types:

- the Idealist
- the Counsellor
- the Enthusiast

Statistical data:

- *mentors* constitute one per cent of the global community and are the most rarely occurring of the sixteen personality types

- women predominate among *mentors* (80 per cent)
- Norway is an example of a nation corresponding to the *mentor's* profile

Find out more!

The Mentor. Your Guide to the INFJ Personality Type by Jaroslaw Jankowski

The Practitioner (ISTP)

Life motto: Actions speak louder than words.

Practitioners are optimistic and spontaneous, with a positive approach to life. Reserved and independent, they hold true to their personal convictions and view external principles and norms with scepticism. They find abstract concepts and solutions for the future tiresome and would far rather roll up their sleeves and get to work on solving tangible and concrete problems.

Adapting well to new places and situations, they enjoy fresh challenges and risks and are capable of keeping a cool head in the face of threats and danger. Their general reticence and extreme reserve when it comes to expressing their opinions mean that other people may often find them impenetrable.

The *practitioner's* four natural inclinations:

- source of life energy: the interior world
- mode of assimilating information: via the senses

- decision-making mode: the mind
- lifestyle: spontaneous

Similar personality types:
- the Inspector
- the Animator
- the Administrator

Statistical data:
- *practitioners* constitute between six and nine per cent of the global community
- men predominate among *practitioners* (60 per cent)
- Singapore is an example of a nation corresponding to the *practitioner's* profile

Find out more!

The Practitioner. Your Guide to the ISTP Personality Type by Jaroslaw Jankowski

The Presenter (ESFP)

Life motto: Now is the perfect moment!

Presenters are optimistic, energetic and outgoing, with the ability to enjoy life and have fun to the full. Practical, flexible and spontaneous at one and the same time, they enjoy change and new experiences, coping badly with solitude, stagnation and routine.

With their liking for being at the centre of attention, they are natural-born actors and their speaking abilities arouse the interest and enthusiasm of their listeners. Focused as they are on the present moment, they will sometimes lose sight of their long-term aims and can also have problems with foreseeing the consequences of their actions.

The *presenter's* four natural inclinations:
- source of life energy: the exterior world
- mode of assimilating information: via the senses
- decision-making mode: the heart
- lifestyle: spontaneous

Similar personality types:
- the Advocate
- the Artist
- the Protector

Statistical data:
- *presenters* constitute between eight and thirteen per cent of the global community
- women predominate among *presenters* (60 per cent)
- Brazil is an example of a nation corresponding to the *presenter's* profile

Find out more!
The Presenter. Your Guide to the ESFP Personality Type by Jaroslaw Jankowski

The Protector (ISFJ)

Life motto: Your happiness matters to me.

Protectors are sincere, warm-hearted, unassuming, trustworthy and extraordinarily loyal. With their ability to perceive people's needs and their desire to help them, they will always put others first. Practical, well-organised and gifted with both an eye and a memory for detail, they are responsible, hard-working, patient, persevering and capable of seeing things through to the end.

Protectors set great store by tranquillity, stability and friendly relations with others and are skilled at building bridges between people. By the same token, they find conflict and criticism difficult to bear. Given their powerful sense of duty and their constant readiness to come to the aid of others, they can end up being used by people.

The *protector's* four natural inclinations:

- source of life energy: the interior world
- mode of assimilating information: via the senses
- decision-making mode: the heart
- lifestyle: organised

Similar personality types:

- the Artist
- the Advocate
- the Presenter

Statistical data:
- *protectors* constitute between eight and twelve per cent of the global population
- women predominate among *protectors* (70 per cent)
- Sweden is an example of a nation corresponding to the *protector's* profile

Find out more!
The Protector. Your Guide to the ISFJ Personality Type by Jaroslaw Jankowski

The Strategist (INTJ)

Life motto: I can certainly improve this.

Strategists are independent and outstandingly individualistic, with an immense seam of inner energy. Creative, inventive and resourceful, others perceive them as competent, self-assured and, at one and the same time, distant and enigmatic. No matter what they turn their attention to, they will always look at the bigger picture and they have a driving urge to improve the world around them and set it in order.

Well-organised, responsible, critical and demanding, they are difficult to knock off balance – and just as hard to please to the full. Reading the emotions and feelings of others is something they find very problematic.

The *strategist's* four natural inclinations:
- source of life energy: the interior world

- mode of assimilating information: intuition
- decision-making mode: the mind
- lifestyle: organised

Similar personality types:
- the Logician
- the Director
- the Innovator

Statistical data:
- *strategists* constitute between one and two per cent of the global community
- men predominate among *strategists* (80 per cent)
- Finland is an example of a nation corresponding to the *strategist's* profile

Find out more!
The Strategist. Your Guide to the INTJ Personality Type by Jaroslaw Jankowski

Additional information

The four natural inclinations

1. THE DOMINANT SOURCE OF LIFE ENERGY

    a. THE EXTERIOR WORLD
       People who draw their energy from outside. They need activity and contact with others and find being alone for any length of time hard to bear.

    b. THE INTERIOR WORLD
       People who draw their energy from their inner world. They need quiet and solitude and feel drained when they spend any length of time in a group.

2. **THE DOMINANT MODE OF ASSIMILATING INFORMATION**

    a. VIA THE SENSES
    People who rely on the five senses and are persuaded by facts and evidence. They have a liking for methods and practices which are tried and tested and prefer concrete tasks and are realists who trust in experience.

    b. VIA INTUITION
    People who rely on the sixth sense and are driven by what they 'feel in their bones'. They have a liking for innovative solutions and problems of a theoretical nature and are characterised by a creative approach to their tasks and the ability to predict.

3. **THE DOMINANT DECISION-MAKING MODE**

    a. THE MIND
    People who are guided by logic and objective principles. They are critical and direct in expressing their opinions.

    b. THE HEART
    People who are guided by their feelings and values. They long for harmony and mutual understanding with others.

ADDITIONAL INFORMATION

4. THE DOMINANT LIFESTYLE

   a. ORGANISED
   People who are conscientious and organised. They value order and like to operate according to plan.

   b. SPONTANEOUS
   People who are spontaneous and value freedom of action. They live for the moment and have no trouble finding their feet in new situations.

The approximate percentage of each personality type in the world population

Personality Type:	**Proportion:**
- The Administrator (ESTJ):	10-13%
- The Advocate (ESFJ):	10-13%
- The Animator (ESTP):	6-10%
- The Artist (ISFP):	6-9%
- The Counsellor (ENFJ):	3-5 %
- The Director (ENTJ):	2-5%
- The Enthusiast (ENFP):	5-8%
- The Idealist (INFP):	1-4%
- The Innovator (ENTP):	3-5%
- The Inspector (ISTJ):	6-10%
- The Logician (INTP):	2-3%
- The Mentor (INFJ):	ca. 1%
- The Practitioner (ISTP):	6-9%
- The Presenter (ESFP):	8-13%

- The Protector (ISFJ): 8-12%
- The Strategist (INTJ): 1-2%

The approximate percentage of women and men of each personality type in the world population

Personality Type: **Women / Men:**

- The Administrator (ESTJ): 40% / 60%
- The Advocate (ESFJ): 70% / 30%
- The Animator (ESTP): 40% / 60%
- The Artist (ISFP): 60% / 40%
- The Counsellor (ENFJ): 80% / 20%
- The Director (ENTJ): 30% / 70%
- The Enthusiast (ENFP): 60% / 40%
- The Idealist (INFP): 60% / 40%
- The Innovator (ENTP): 30% / 70%
- The Inspector (ISTJ): 40% / 60%
- The Logician (INTP): 20% / 80%
- The Mentor (INFJ): 80% / 20%
- The Practitioner (ISTP): 40% / 60%
- The Presenter (ESFP): 60% / 40%
- The Protector (ISFJ): 70% / 30%
- The Strategist (INTJ): 20% / 80%

Bibliography

- Arraj, Tyra & Arraj, James: *Tracking the Elusive Human, Volume 1: A Practical Guide to C.G. Jung's Psychological Types, W.H. Sheldon's Body and Temperament Types and Their Integration*, Inner Growth Books, 1988
- Arraj, James: *Tracking the Elusive Human, Volume 2: An Advanced Guide to the Typological Worlds of C. G. Jung, W.H. Sheldon, Their Integration, and the Biochemical Typology of the Future*, Inner Growth Books, 1990
- Berens, Linda V.; Cooper, Sue A.; Ernst, Linda K.; Martin, Charles R.; Myers, Steve; Nardi, Dario; Pearman, Roger R.; Segal, Marci; Smith, Melissa: *A Quick Guide to the 16 Personality Types in Organizations: Understanding Personality Differences in the Workplace*, Telos Publications, 2002
- Geier, John G. & Downey, E. Dorothy: *Energetics of Personality*, Aristos Publishing House, 1989
- Hunsaker, Phillip L. & Alessandra, Anthony J.: *The Art of Managing People*, Simon and Schuster, 1986
- Jung, Carl Gustav: *Psychological Types (The Collected Works of C. G. Jung, Vol. 6)*, Princeton University Press, 1976

- Kise, Jane A. G.; Stark, David & Krebs Hirsch, Sandra: *LifeKeys: Discover Who You Are*, Bethany House, 2005
- Kroeger, Otto & Thuesen, Janet: *Type Talk or How to Determine Your Personality Type and Change Your Life*, Delacorte Press, 1988
- Lawrence, Gordon: *People Types and Tiger Stripes*, Center for Applications of Psychological Type, 1993
- Lawrence, Gordon: *Looking at Type and Learning Styles*, Center for Applications of Psychological Type, 1997
- Maddi, Salvatore R.: *Personality Theories: A Comparative Analysis*, Waveland, 2001
- Martin, Charles R.: *Looking at Type: The Fundamentals Using Psychological Type To Understand and Appreciate Ourselves and Others*, Center for Applications of Psychological Type, 2001
- Meier C.A.: Personality: *The Individuation Process in the Light of C. G. Jung's Typology*, Daimon Verlag, 2007
- Pearman, Roger R. & Albritton, Sarah: *I'm Not Crazy, I'm Just Not You: The Real Meaning of the Sixteen Personality Types*, Davies-Black Publishing, 1997
- Segal, Marci: Creativity and Personality Type: *Tools for Understanding and Inspiring the Many Voices of Creativity*, Telos Publications, 2001
- Sharp, Daryl: Personality Type: *Jung's Model of Typology*, Inner City Books, 1987
- Spoto, Angelo: *Jung's Typology in Perspective*, Chiron Publications, 1995
- Tannen, Deborah: *You Just Don't Understand*, William Morrow and Company, 1990
- Thomas, Jay C. & Segal, Daniel L.: *Comprehensive Handbook of Personality and Psychopathology, Personality and Everyday Functioning*, Wiley, 2005
- Thomson, Lenore: *Personality Type: An Owner's Manual*, Shambhala, 1998
- Tieger, Paul D. & Barron-Tieger Barbara: *Just Your Type: Create the Relationship You've Always Wanted Using the Secrets of Personality Type*, Little, Brown and Company, 2000
- Von Franz, Marie-Louise & Hillman, James: *Lectures on Jung's Typology*, Continuum International Publishing Group, 1971

www.ingramcontent.com/pod-product-compliance
Lightning Source LLC
Chambersburg PA
CBHW031209020426
42333CB00013B/851